# KNOW ABOUT
# TIPU SULTAN

MAPLE KIDS

KNOW ABOUT  TIPU SULTAN

Published by

MAPLE PRESS PRIVATE LIMITED
office: A-63, Sector 58, Noida 201301, U.P., India
phone: +91 120 455 3581, 455 3583
email: info@maplepress.co.in
website: www.maplepress.co.in

Reprinted in 2019

ISBN: 978-93-50334-16-4

# Contents

Preface ................................................................ 4

1. Birth of Tipu Sultan .................................... 6

2. Re-establishment of Sringeri.................... 10

3. Religious Prospect.................................... 13

4. The French Connection............................ 17

5. Policies of Tipu ......................................... 20

6. Mysore ....................................................... 24

7. A Tiger Trail Warrior................................. 27

8. Hyder Ali ................................................... 30

9. Seringapatam ............................................ 34

10. Fall of The Tiger........................................ 38

11. Social System ........................................... 41

12. Trade and Commerce .............................. 44

13. Peculiar Justice......................................... 48

14. Social Reformer ........................................ 51

15. Revolutionary Principles ......................... 54

16. Commercial Relations ............................. 57

17. External Policy.......................................... 63

18. Afghanistan and Iran .............................. 66

19. Political Liberty ........................................ 69

20. Technology................................................ 71

21. Tipu's Government................................... 74

22. Timeline of Tipu's Life ............................. 76

23. Tipu's Skill ................................................ 79

# Preface

After his father Hyder Ali's death (1782), Tipu Sultan assumed power in Mysore. Tipu's avowed aim was to banish the British from his kingdom. Tipu had great interest in science & technology and highly promoted trade & commerce in his state. Progressive aspects of his rule included the development of sericulture, breeding the fine Seringapatam Ox, building tanks and dams to control monsoon flooding and to promote agriculture, the application of European military technology and a keen awareness of the politics of secularism. He wanted to bring up Mysore as the most developed & powerful state of India.

Many historians have regarded Tipu's rule as one that fostered secular and liberal views. An interesting aspect of Tipu's life was that he was founder member of the Jacobin Club. He then proceeded to call himself 'Citizen Tipu Sultan', a radical shift in the policy of an Indian ruler, among his contemporaries who in general, tolerated no liberal or socialist opinions.

This book sums up the events of Tipu Sultan with an account of the wars that he fought along with his achievements as ruler.

# CHAPTER 1
# Birth of Tipu Sultan

Hyder Ali was the ruler of Mysore. Tipu Sultan was his eldest son. He took birth on December 10, 1750 at Devanahalli. From childhood onwards, he got training in the art of battle. Even at the young age of fifteen, he accompanied his father, Hyder Ali, to many military movements. He was very good in studies. He knew different languages and he was also interested in other subjects like Mathematics and Science. Tipu

Sultan had a strong interest for learning. He had a personal library that consisted of more than 2,000 books in various languages. He was a very powerful man who toiled hard for the welfare of his subjects. In the year 1782, his father died of a skin infection. At that time, he was in the middle of a battle against the British. So, Tipu Sultan had to take over the empire of Mysore after the death of his father.

### Ideals of Tipu Sultan

Tipu had a creative vision to bring about a social and economic change in the life of the people. He was able to enhance the prestige and wealth of his state. He brought about reforms in every department of life, like currency and calendar, weights and measures, banking and finance, trade and commerce, agriculture and industry, morals and manners and social and cultural life. If he had not been engaged intensely maddening wars, he would definitely have led his empire into a revolutionary stage. He had a well-organized administration. He was perhaps the first Indian ruler to apply western techniques in his government. He applied modern measures and new policies that helped Mysore gain almost international importance of his times. He achieved all this because he was progressive, patriotic and worldly in character.

Tipu inherited the secular policy of Hyder Ali who was very open-minded in religious affairs. Tipu walked on his father's footsteps, though he was much more religious than Hyder.

There are about thirty letters in Kannada of Tipu to Swamiji of Sringeri temple. They were found in 1916 by R.Narasimhachar, Director of Archaeology in Mysore. Normally, all letters of Tipu to others used to begin with his own name at the top, but these letters mentioned the name of Swamiji at the top, with all his titles and Tipu's name at the bottom without any title. These letters explain the depth of his religious policy and plainly establish the secular character of his rule.

*"The Quran requires you to say to people of scripture: We believe in that which has been revealed into us and revealed unto you, our God*

*and your God is one and unto him we surrender. We hold this God-given law dear to our heart, based as it is on human dignity, reason and brotherhood of man. With reverence we have also read the Vedas of the Hindus. They proclaim their faith in universal unity and express the belief that God is one although He bears many names."* Tipu Sultan.

# CHAPTER 2
# Re-establishment of Sringeri

In the year 1791, the Maratha army caused a lot of damage to Sringeri. Parshuram Bhau was the leader of the army. The army looted the property of the temple and the sacred image of Goddess Sharada was also shifted. Swamiji of the temple had to leave the place and went to Karkala in Dakshina Kannada District. Swamiji informed Tipu, about the raid of Marathas and sought for his help in order to purify the holy image of the Goddess. Tipu gave an immediate reaction to the request and wrote to Sri Shankaracharya, the Swamiji of the temple, expressing sentiments of respect for Hinduism and thus denied any charge of racism pointed against him. He provided Swamiji with funds to reinstall the displaced image and thus ordered the Assaf (Collector) of Bidnur to supply both cash and other useful articles.

He also expressed his sorrow at the ill-fated incidents, which resulted in the destruction of the holy place. In one of these letters, Tipu cited a Sanskrit verse, which said, "people commit evil deeds smilingly but they would later regret for them weepingly."

In another record; it is specified that- Tipu sent two palanquins, one for the Goddess and another for Swamiji.

These letters depict high values and respect to the holy place and to Swamiji. This treatment didn't confine only to the phase when Tipu was fighting a battle with Marathas but it extended throughout his rule. At another time, when there was no war, Tipu addressed Swamiji as 'Jagadguru' and requested him to pray for the interests and happiness of all the people.

Sringeri was not the only holy place, which received the aid and patronage of Tipu.

To the Lakshmikantha temple at Kalale in Nanjangud taluk of Mysore district, he gave four silver cups, a silver plate and a silver spittoon. To the Narayanaswamy temple at Melkote, he presented gold and silver vessels besides an elephant and a few jewels.

# CHAPTER 3
# Religious Prospect

The Srikanteswara temple at Nanjangud was presented with a jeweled cup along with few precious stones. Together which he also presented an emerald necklace and a 'Linga' of Jade to be enshrined in the temple. There was another famous temple known as Ranganatha temple, which was very close to his palace. This temple still stands there and it was presented seven silver cups and silver camphor banners by him.

In 1774, when a part of this temple got damaged in a fire, it was rebuilt within a month. Tipu never discriminated between the ringing of the bells from the temple and the call of Azan from the mosque.

There were two other temples near the mosque, the Narasimha temple and the Gangadhareshwara temple where daily 'pujas' were performed without any interference. He fixed an allowance to the temple at Rayakottai. By paying 10,000 huns, he ordered the completion of the temple of Gopur in Conjeevaram whose foundations had been laid in 1780 by Hyder. As Hyder died before the completion of the temple, Tipu not only ordered its completion but also participated in its opening ceremony. When a dispute arose in Melkote due to some religious assumptions, he sent his good staff to settle the issue. Finally, both the parties agreed and he solved the problem to the satisfaction of both.

Tipu was impartial and fair to all his subjects.

He had employed many Hindus at high posts and acted fairly with all religion without any discrimination. Purnaiya was the minister-in-charge of the important Department of Revenue and Finance. Krishna Rao was the treasurer, Shama lyengaar was incharge of Law and Order and Police. Narasing Rao and Ranga lyengaar held key posts in Srirangapatna, Srinivasa Rao and Appaji Ram were the main diplomats who discussed peace and war with external powers. Mool Chand and Sajjan Rai were his chief agents at the Mughal court in Delhi. Nagappaiah, a *brahmin*, was the faujdar of Coorg. His civil list is full of the names of Hindus who held important posts in the state.

Hindus were assigned with many important and responsible jobs in the army also. Hari Singh commanded a division of combat troop. Sripat Rao was appointed with Roshan Khan to contain the rebellious Nayars in Malabar. Shivaji, a Maratha, held the command of 3000 horses and defended Bangalore against the attack of Lord Cornwallis in the Third Mysore

War. Tipu encouraged the Armenian Christian merchants to come and settle in Mysore and provided them with all the facilities to promote mutual trade.

# CHAPTER 4
# The French Connection

Tipu selected people for services strictly on their merits. He didn't consider any other factor. He mentioned in one of his letters, "God bestows power on those who are worthy of his trust irrespective of caste, creed or colour." He had strict watch on those Muslim saints who used to attract followers to their own ways of religious thoughts. He also terminated some of the rituals practised by Muslims in the month of Muharram.

He enforced ban on his subjects- Hindus, Muslims and Christians from taking liquor.

Tipu was very much interested in the revolutionary ideas of France that penetrated his court through the French officers. This was also one of the important features of Tipu's policy that clearly brings out the secular and progressive character of his administration. He communicated with the French, welcomed their modem and revolutionary ideas and implemented western techniques of warfare and system of administration. The French soldiers commanded by M. Dompart, who was in Tipu's service, formed a Jacobin Club of extreme revolutionary ideas of liberty, equality and fraternity at Srirangapatna. There were 59 members in this club and Tipu himself was one of them. This club was formed on May 5, 1797, the fifth year of the French Republic. The aim of this club was to communicate instructions in constitutional principles of democratic nature and for farming laws similar to those existing in the Republic of France. While accepting the membership, Tipu declared, "Behold my acknowledgement of the standard of your country, which is dear to me and to which I am connected, it shall always be supported in my country, as it has been in the Republic, my sister!"

# CHAPTER 5
# Policies of Tipu

Tipu was much ahead of his times and was known as the modernizer. He was charged with religious intolerance, which seemed to be illogical. The English, who had suffered imprisonment at his hands, blamed him due to their hostility towards him. But the notable fact is that they forgot that the sufferings of the English prisoners were only the sufferings of those who had tried to destroy him. His harshness towards his enemies was based on political grounds and not religious.

This fact could be supported by the conditions he specified in his proposed 'Treaty of Alliance with French', which declared," I demand that male and female prisoners as well as English and Portuguese, who shall be taken by the republican troops or by mine, shall be treated with humanity and with regard to their persons that they shall be transported at our joint expense out of India to some place far distant from the territories of the allies."

Such thoughts certainly show his humanity within, even to those who were his hardened enemies. Such a person could hardly be unkind to his own subjects, no matter to what religion they belonged.

Gandhiji wrote in 'Young India' that, "Tipu Sultan was a representation of Hindu-Muslim Unity. No Indian ruler, who did not enjoy the confidence of his own people, could have fought three frantic wars with a European Power." He was very famous with his army and his people.

He was greatly interested in Sufism, the liberal trend in Islam, which just believed in the unity of God and the unity of Man. He held the Hindu saints, Sadhus and Gods in high regard. He consulted Hindu astrologers. He fed the *brahmins* and bore the expenses of the Hindu ceremonies.

If he crushed the Hindus of Coorg, the Christians of Mangalore and the Nayars of Malabar, who were supporting the English to weaken his power, he did not spare the Muslim Mopillas and Mahadevis in the interest of Law and Order and to improve the condition of his state. He attacked the Nawab of Savanur, threatened the Muslim ruler of Kurnool and was more hostile towards the Nizam and the Nawab of Carnatic than towards the Marathas. At times, his harshness was politically motivated and was not at all based on religious factors. Tipu's sense of respect for Hindus could be guessed by the fact that he did not attack the Dindigal fort from the back, as a temple was there. When somebody suggested to him that

Purnaiya's loyalty was suspected and that the *brahmin* community was unreliable, he always uttered a Quranic verse which prohibited the blaming of the whole community for the fault of one. When an officer reported to him that a Hindu had married a Muslim girl, he scolded the officer and warned him not to raise such personal issues.

# CHAPTER 6
# Mysore

On getting to power, Tipu realized that the new political development that had taken place in the country, had disturbed the traditional balance of power in the land completely. Without the re-establishment of that balance, there would be a loss of the National identity. He was now aware that the British wanted to crush the sovereignty of Indian rulers and reduce them to the positions of a pensioned Nawabs or Rajas.

Long before the events of 1857 and before the formation of the Indian National Congress, which accelerated the pace of Nationalist Movement, Tipu slogged hard to rouse an awareness of his neighbours to the approaching danger to Indian Independence from the English.

Tipu looked for the support of Indian powers, especially the Marathas and the Nizam. When he saw that the response was not satisfying, he focused his attention to external help like from France, Turkey, Iran, Paris, Constantinople or Afghanistan.

As a result, his kingdom, otherwise small in size, extent and resources, was dragged into the whirlpool of world politics and achieved the stature of global importance. His name would be taken in England to scare the naughty children. His ambassadors would receive grand reception in Paris, Constantinople and Kabul. Mysore had become 'the terror of Leaden Hall Street' the head quarters of East India Company in London. His commercial depots were positioned all over in West Asia. He made the status of Mysore very high.

Under Tipu's leadership, the Mysore army became a model and a school of military science to Indian powers.

# CHAPTER 7
# A Tiger Trail Warrior

Tipu caused great disappointment to the Governor of Madras (Chennai), to the Nawab of Carnatic, Muhammad Ali when he tried to capture them in the country house in the Company's garden. A small vessel, that by accident was opposite the garden, furnished them with the means of escaping. Thus, it was a fortunate escape of the whole Madras government, which were about to be captured by Tipu, who had been in independent command of a body of troops in the First Mysore War.

The fight continued for a year and half, in which the British suffered heavy losses. Hyder recovered Mangalore and so the panic-stricken British had to sue for peace. A treaty was signed on April 4, 1769, on the basis of restitution of each other's territories. It was also a defensive alliance, as the English promised to help Hyder, in case he was attacked by any other power.

However, the terms of the treaty were not fulfilled by the Madras Government. The British refused to help Hyder Ali when Mysore was attacked by the Marathas in 1771. Hyder found that the French gave him more support in terms of his military demands. So in 1780, when the English wanted to attack the French at Mahe, situated on the west coast of Mysore, Hyder Ali did not authorize it. Therefore the English declared war against Hyder Ali.

Tipu accompanied his father in this battle as well. Hyder Ali arranged a joint front with the Nizam and the Marathas. In July 1780, Hyder Ali along with 80,000 men and 100 guns attacked Carnatic. In October 1780, he captured Arcot, defeating English army under Colonel William Braille. Tipu Sultan was in such anger on Colonel Bailey, that the entire English army was either cut or taken prisoners. Bailey himself suffered for long in the prisons of Srirangapatna.

# CHAPTER 8
# Hyder Ali

Hyder Ali was fearless and he continued with the war against the British courageously. Hyder Ali was defeated by Sir Eyre Coote at Porto Nova in November 1781. Trincomali, the harbour of Ceylon was captured by the English in January 1782. In the year 1782, Hyder Ali inflicted a humiliating defeat on the British troops under Colonel Braithwaite. But Hyder Ali was not destined to fight more. Hyder Ali died on

December 7, 1782 and left the unfinished task to his son Tipu Sultan.

Upon becoming Sultan after his father's death in 1782, Tipu worked to check British advances through a series of association. He became convinced that the British were a new kind of threat in India. At first, he attempted to secure pacts with the Marathas and the Mughal Empire.

Like his father, Tipu Sultan was a brave warrior and continued the war against the British. Brigadier Mathews, appointed by the Bombay (Mumbai) Government was captured by Tipu in 1783. Then in November 1783, Colonel William Fullarton captured Coimbatore.

But absolute success eluded both the sides. Tired of the war, the two sides concluded the 'Treaty of Mangalore' in 1784. According to the treaty, both the parties decided to restore each other's conquered territories and free all the prisoners. Thus, even the second round of struggle proved inconclusive. Warren Hastings, however, did not like the terms of treaty and the British did not gain anything from the war.

The Treaty of Mangalore of 1784 between Tipu Sultan and the English was nothing but a hollow ceasefire. When Lord Cornwallis came to India, he was bound by the 'Pitt's India Act' to refrain from following a policy of war, except for purely defensive purpose. Tipu Sultan was also not satisfied by the treaty of 1784 and so in 1787 sent an agent to France and Constantinople for support. Cornwallis believed that Tipu if united himself with the French would strike against the English. So he worked on the anti-Tipu suspicions of the Nizams and Marathas. Cornwallis provoked Tipu by signing an agreement with the Nizams for help to recover the district of Balaghat, which was in the possession of Mysore.

The immediate cause of the war was Tipu's attack on Travancore on December 29, 1789. Tipu's differences with the Raja of Travancore arose over the latter's purchase of Jaikottai and Travancore from the Dutch in the Cochin state and Tipu considered Cochin as his tributary state and thus considered the act of the Raja as violation of his sovereign rights. On the other hand, the Raja of Travancore was entitled to the protection of the English. Thus, taking advantage of this situation, the English made a triple union by joining with the Nizams and the Marathas and attacked Tipu Sultan.

# CHAPTER 9
# Seringapatam (Now known as Srirangapatna)

Major General Medows was not able to give any decisive results. On the other hand, Tipu demonstrated greater skills and strategies than Medows. Cornwallis himself took over the command of the British troops on January 29, 1791. Cornwallis proceeded through Vellore and Ambure to Bangalore along with a large army. In the year 1791, he captured Bangalore. Then on May 31, he approached Tipu's capital Seringapatam. Tipu displayed great skill in defending and his tactics forced Cornwallis to retreat by cutting off supplies. General Medows and Lord Cornwallis were harassed for two long years.

The fighting was resumed in the summer of 1791. Tipu captured Coimbatore on November 3. But, Cornwallis, with the help of the army sent from Bombay, occupied all the forts in his path to Seringapatam, where he arrived on February 5, 1792. Tipu displayed all his skills and offered tough resistance but soon realized the impossibility of earning from the struggle further. But only an All India Confederacy of the Nizam, the Maratha and the English together with a secret entry into Seringapatam in the dead of night enabled the opponents to beat Tipu.

Tipu had to sue for peace and the Treaty of Seringapatam concluded in March 1792. The treaty resulted in the surrender of nearly half of the territory of Mysore to the victorious allies. The British acquired Baramahal, Dindigul and Malabar while the Marathas got territory on the Tungabhadra side and the Nizams acquired the territories from the Krishna to beyond the Pennar. Tipu also had to pay a war compensation of over three million pounds and hand over his two sons as hostages.

Out of this war, the Company gained some possessions in the South, which added to the strength and compactness of the Company's territories. Cornwallis summed up the Company's gains, "We have effectively crippled our enemy without making our friends too powerful."

Lord Wellesley was an imperialist and combined the instruments of war and supremacy. Wellesley was determined either to tame Tipu to submission or wipe out Tipu's independence. Out of this grew the system of Subsidiary Alliances. He developed this system as part of a bid for more effective British supremacy. The system was such that when an

Indian ruler was in danger of his neighbours, they could take help of the English and in return they would have to pay and maintain the British troops in his state. This system was a complete success. It undermined the independence of Indian rulers and made the British power gain superiority in India.

# CHAPTER 10
# Fall of The Tiger

Tipu Sultan made attempts to secure an association with the French against the English in India. He sent ambassadors to Arabia, Kabul, Constantinople, Versailles and Mauritius. Tipu's proposals were welcomed by the French Governor. A proclamation was published that invited volunteers so as to come forward to assist Tipu. Therefore in April, 1798, some Frenchmen landed in Mangalore. On the other hand, Wellesley apprehended danger from Tipu. Thus he moved to Madras and made attempts to segregate Tipu Sultan by reviving the Triple Alliance. Arthur Wellesley, the duke of Wellington, who later became the defeater of Napoleon, was harassed greatly and was forced to join the camp of General Harris. The Nizams agreed to conclude subsidiary treaties with English on September 1, 1798. However, the Marathas turned down the British's offer and remained reserved and neutral.

Following all these arrangements, Wellesley called upon Tipu to question the relationship with the French. Tipu's explanation that, 'only 40 persons, French and of dark colour, of whom 10 or 12 were skilled persons and the rest servants paid the fare of the ship, came here in search of employment', did not satisfy Wellesley. Thus, two British forces, one from Bombay and the other from Madras, fell upon Mysore.

The fourth Anglo-Mysore War was of very short duration and decisive. Tipu was defeated by Stuart at Sedaseer on March 5, 1799 and by General Harris at Malvelly on March 27. Tipu then retired to Seringapatam, which was finally captured on May 4, 1799. Tipu was killed fighting bravely. Thus fell a leading Indian power and one of the most established foes of the English. The members of Tipu's family were interned at Vellore. The English annexed Kanara, Coimbatore, Wynad and Dharpouram besides the entire sea coast of Mysore. The Nizams received some land, which they handed over again to the Company for the support of the British troops.

Thus, the fourth Mysore war destroyed the whole state of Mysore. The British also offered some territories to Peshwas, which they did not accept. Mysore was restored to the Hindu royal family after signing a subsidiary alliance. In addition to the usual provisions, the Governor General could interfere with the administration. As a result of this war, the British got complete power of South India. After this war, Wellesley was given the title of Marquees by the British Government.

# CHAPTER 11
## Social System

Tipu used to think much ahead of his times. The significant feature of his life was his attentiveness of the 18th Century world's realities. He saw the development in terms of inventions and discoveries, explorations and voyages, new learning and renaissance of Europe.

The nervous system of the body of Indian politics had been blocked by only one type of authority and dictatorship. Caste system had paralyzed the social system. The tendency of each rank or state to declare its own authority had divided the land. Tipu made efforts to balance the situation and built up faithfulness to a larger state.

His concept of a nation-state, his sense of responsibility to the needs of the people, his removal of feudal mediators and his building up of a standard system of law and efficient system of administration were all modern ideas far ahead of his times.

These ideas were afterwards adopted by those who were earlier against them. Tipu's sharp mind quickly recognized that the European Mercantilism was essentially a system of political power. Its intention was to absorb the wealth of other nations through exchange of goods at overpriced rate of profit. The merchandise of the East was sold in western markets, a hundred times more than the actual price. Very quickly, Europe started living on Asia, Africa and America. When Tipu noticed this phenomenon, he tried to change it.

Tipu was a great ruler. Despite the political differences, he had great respect for western science, technology, discipline, organization and system.

Although Tipu was always preoccupied with the hectic political and military concerns, he never ignored the main task of improving the life and condition of his people. He undertook many measures to remove the economic differences. He made a plan of state capitalism. His commercial regulations visualized a scheme of banking organization in which small investors received a higher profit. It was a test of a new type of Cooperative Bank that promoted small savings. To build up this banking system, he launched the state control of trade, commerce and industries. Mysore was abundant, in commercial crops such as silk, sandalwood, pepper, cardamom, coconut, elephants, ivory and so on. These commercial crops were very much in demand in the Western markets. Tipu was dedicated not to let the trade of these goods fall into foreign hands.

# CHAPTER 12
# Trade and Commerce

Mysore became the greatest exporter of goods, which were being sent out and the importer of the goods, which were being brought in, by its own navy of commercial ships. The hold of private bankers, moneylenders and middlemen was minimized. Tipu developed interests not only in trade and commerce, but also in arts and crafts for state control. There were a large number of workshops, which were set up to manufacture guns, muskets, glass, cannon, paper, cutlery, cloth, sugar and a host of other articles. He had always thought to keep Mysore to be in the front line of shipbuilding industry.

He made a navy both for trade and war. In 1793, he ordered 100 ships to be built with the native material. He concentrated on the making of arms and ammunitions. The factory at Srirangapatna converted iron into steel and manufactured weapons. He called his iron-works as Taramandals, which were four in number, at Srirangapatna, Bangalore, Chitradurga and Bidnur. A machine was planned which bored big guns with power generated by flow of water. Hyder and Tipu's names are outlined notably as the creators of rockets.

The small state of Mysore was linked with the bigger world by the continuous efforts of Tipu. He improved the agriculture and industry, promoted the trade and commerce, designed a new system of the administration of justice, opened new factories and embassies were shifted to different and remote lands. He made a very efficient system of administration, which would change his State into a buzzing centre of big Industrial activities. He applied his utmost to bring artists and craftsmen from various countries so as to manufacture guns, muskets and a host of other goods.

More significant than Tipu's patriotic eagerness was his creative vision, which aimed at bringing about a social change in the condition of the people, in the improvement of the economic life of the masses and in the enrichment of the prestige and prosperity of his state.

He made reforms in almost every section of life including coinage and calendar, weights and measures, banking and finance, revenue and judiciary, army and navy, morals and manners and social culture and cultural affairs.

Tipu Sultan's constant involvement in wars made his state lack the revolutionary stage. He built up an efficient system administration and was almost the first Indian ruler to apply western techniques in the heart of government.

His new measures and energetic policies made Mysore gain almost international importance in his times. All this would never have been possible if he was not powerful and worldly in his character.

# CHAPTER 13
# Peculiar Justice

The silk industry in Karnataka is originated by Tipu Sultan. The state also traded in goods like gold, tobacco, sandalwood, precious metals, elephants, pepper and timber during Tipu's reign. He did set up a Cooperative Bank for money transfer. His administration of justice was linked to such an environment, where the offenders were made to plant trees and nurture them.

For small crimes, such plants were recommended which would grow fast and for serious crimes, those that would take long, like plum, mango and coconut. Many attempts were made to set up pearl-fisheries in Malabar by inviting divers from Muscat. Chinese helped in the production of fine-quality sugar.

A French engineer designed an engine run

by water for bong big guns called cannons. Thus his vision was ahead of his times. He structured a Board of Admiralty, which controlled a navy of 22 lines of battle ships and 20 large sailing warships with 72 and 62 guns respectively and also a navy of merchant ships.

He was having a keen interest in agriculture. He planned to construct a dam exactly on the same location where the present Krishnarajasagar Dam stands today. During the war against the Marathas and the Nizam, he issued orders to watch over the silk worms, which were being brought from Bengal. He paid too much interest towards Sericulture. He was so fond of Horticulture and gardening that all his communication with foreign personage would always carry a request for new varieties of seeds and plants. He altered the tenure of land that enabled the farmers to possess the land. Wastelands were free of rent for farming. He stopped the farming of the land to the highest offerer of money and employed revenue officers to collect the returns. He removed the funding of 'jagirs'. He brought up 'takavi' loans, which supported the farmers in lean seasons. He did not encouraged existing forced labour but encouraged the villagers to settle the disputes among themselves in order to discourage the unnecessary legal actions. It was his great liking for horticulture that made him introduce a new idea to punish the criminals. For various crimes committed by the people, he fixed fair punishment. The punishment was not to impose fine nor to put them behind bars, but to make them plant trees, water them and bring them up to a particular height.

In order to promote agriculture, he introduced industries, promoted trade and commerce on a large scale.

# CHAPTER 14
# Social Reformer

He was a great social reformer. He banned liquor and the use of tobacco. He stopped the purchase and sale of abandoned girls and children. He also put checks on the open-handed expenses on the celebrations of weddings. He was also responsible for bringing other social reforms. He used to be very fair while delivering justice. Once he punished his eldest son, Fateh Hyder, who took vegetables without asking the owner.

He set up the first newspaper, Fauji Akhbar. Tipu Sultan himself was an author. He knew many languages like Urdu, Persian, Arabic, Kannada, Marathi, English and French. More than 45 books were written during his time. His library consisted of 2000 manuscripts, one of them being the hand written Quran by Aurangazeb. He got a huge album prepared showing the pictures of all great Sufi saints both from India and abroad.

Tipu had a first concern list in which 'Freedom of the land' was on the top. He turned the resources of his state first to protect and preserve the freedom, as any sacrifice was too small for its protection. The weapons were very significant because without them neither he nor his state could survive. Tipu evaluated the tendency of Western political and economic development that aimed at weakening Indian economy so as to suit imperial interests.

Instead of surrendering to foreign forces, Tipu tried to present a model of his own idea. If this idea had been given an opportunity, it would have given him good results.

This model was to join the western trade on the structure of Indian economy by removing the harmful effects of native feudalism and by giving a powerful push to the growth of Indian capitalism. Tipu played a unique role among all the Indian rulers in the sphere of economic policies and measures. He brought about independent changes in all the aspects of economy, whether agriculture, trade or industry.

# CHAPTER 15
# Revolutionary Principles

Tipu was revolutionist in thought and action. He always struggled against cowardice, unfairness and ignorance. He always had something new in his restless mind. He wanted to educate his masses faster than they could learn. He had a passion for creation and a desire for modernization.

His message for the future generations:-

- One should live and die for a cause. The cause Tipu lived and died for was liberty, which is the soul of history.

- There is no security in life, there are only opportunities. Those who make the best use of the opportunity, as he did, would live in history.

- He taught us that one should not cut a tree to get the fruit. The unstable authorities of his times indulged too much in the process of destroying their own garden instead of making it grow. Whether it was the Nizam or the Marathas, they thought of their own gain and not of the land.

- Tipu was aware that India was a gold mine of limitless resources, which needed to be tapped to make her people happy & prosperous. He struggled all his life to properly control & utilize the resources of the land, so that the people could be happy.

- Tipu's life reminds us that the need of the hour at all times was to shake off disunity and lack of interest. He set himself a good example of being powerful, inventive and creative. His fertile, restless and resourceful mind gave birth to so many projects that made him stand as a superior. He always followed the fact that man should rise from the vain pleasures of life and work for inner development of oneself which is the true destiny. Forces were at work during his times, which stood in the way of development and he wanted to clear the path for these developments. Many great personalities of the world have remained enshrined in the heart of generation next and have become bright stars on the horizon of human heritage. This is the inner-reality that is explicit in Tipu's life. It was his death that made him immortal.

# CHAPTER 16
# Commercial Relations

Mysore had good harbour and there was an abundant production of some important goods like pepper, cardamom, sandalwood, ivory, silk and tobacco. Mysore was also into the trading of elephants, which had great demand outside. Tipu also made commercial relations with a number of foreign countries such as Ottoman Empire, China, Muscat, Peru, Armenia, Jeddah ormuz and Basra. But for him the political contacts were more important than these commercial relations.

In the 18th Century, Turkey was a strong force and had resisted Russian expansion and held vast territories in Eastern Europe. Tipu saw the expanding influence of the British as a threat to entire Islamic world and called the English 'the enemies of faith'. He wanted the Turkish Sultan to direct a campaign against the Europeans. For this purpose, Tipu sent an official to Constantinople in 1784 named Usman Khan.

He got a positive response from there and so he sent another four more officials in 1785.

His purpose was to conclude a political and military treaty against the English. Tipu wrote a letter to Sultan Abdul Hameed, in which, he told him about the British and what they committed in India and asked for the military support. The fourth article of the proposed treaty spoke of military co-operation between Mysore and Turkey.

Another clause said that, 'give as many

technicians as possible to help Tipu in gun and cannon making'. Tipu said that the negligence in commerce and industry was the main cause of their fall in the East.

The ambassadors were given a warm welcome in Constantinople, but the main issue of the treaty was avoided. Sultan Abdul Hameed said that the Russians had set their eyes on the Ottoman Empire and he was engaged in resisting their threat. The British had craftily utilized this weakness of Turkey to keep it on their side and the Turks would not push away the English at a time when Russia was at their door. The officials came back to India empty-handed.

Tipu was having very close relations with France. He was very hopeful to get their support, because of their historic role in the American war of Independence and which had removed the English from their thirteen rich colonies in the new world. Moreover, Tipu was very well aware of the fact that the British were trying to establish their kingdom in India by making one prince fight with another. This feature of the western method of divide and rule made Tipu to apply same technique and thus he persuaded the French, who were the fixed opponents of the English. The Anglo-French hatred was there since the days of Crecy and Agincourt. This hatred lasted all through the centuries until the First World War of 1914.

So the enmity to the British was one common reason between the French and Tipu, who viewed themselves as natural friends. The English were making the Indians fight against the Indians, likewise Tipu too would make the Europeans fight against the Europeans. There were some specific advantages in such a policy, for the Indians would get a breathing space, both western powers would get tired, both would look for Indian support and in the confusion either of the two European powers would be erased. If the English were to be erased, it would be good for India.

In the struggle for dominance, the Dutch had removed the Portuguese and the English had removed the Dutch from India but the French and English were still present. And Tipu was very much aware of this fact. The French were not as weak as the Portuguese or the Dutch and their support had proved decisive in the new world. The presence of a French regiment in his army, their influence at his court, their regular support to Mysore since Hyder Ali's days and a regular visit of French adventures to his capital, gave Tipu high hopes that the drama of American war of independence could be repeated in India.

But the French in India had disappointed Tipu in his expectation of close co-operation. Therefore, he thought of approaching their superiors in Paris. The French adventurers at Tipu's court encouraged him to hope for efficient help if he sent an official to the court of Louis XVI .Therefore in July 1787, three officials with 45 men sailed for Europe from Pondicherry. Tipu asked for 10,000 troops to serve under his direct command. The first article of the proposed treaty stated that war was to be declared against the English and was to be fought until the capture of Madras (Chennai), Bombay (Mumbai) and Bengal. The South was to be conquered first and then the North. The officials reached Toulon in June 1788. The French king had sent his officials to receive them. Tipu's officials were welcomed with great reception.

# CHAPTER 17
# External Policy

The chief theme of external policy of Tipu Sultan was that there had been a new political development in India. This had totally disturbed the traditional power in the land. The national identity would be lost if the balance is not restored. He was the only figure of 18th century who was able to make out the true intentions of the British. This was to reduce the Indian rulers to the position of pensioned Nawabs or Rajas.

The two main intentions of his foreign policy were as follows:

1. To gain military and political assistance from abroad so as to get rid of the British from India.
2. To establish economic contacts so as to promote the well beings of his people at home.

Tipu's external relations were that of seeking help of foreign powers against English. He sent his officials to different countries with letters asking for friendship. He also invited Zaman Shah of Afghanistan to rescue the Mughals from English hand. His relation with Napoleon was very well focused in history. He also encouraged trade and commerce along with political relationship.

### Republic vision

Tipu was not able to get military help from France, yet he was regularly in contact with the French telling them that there was yet a golden chance for them to restore their influence in India if they took a firm decision and stood firmly behind him. But until Napoleon came to power, all his appeals were in vain. Napoleon understood that Tipu could be an effective instrument in forcing the English out of India. He wrote to Tipu from Egypt in 1798 to wait until his arrival in India for a major revolution that might liberate the Indians from the English bondage. He assured Tipu that he would surely help him to realize his dreams. But in the meantime, other factors plotted to defeat the whole scheme. Napoleon himself was beaten at Accre in Syria, which forced him to escape to France quietly. But Tipu was determined to serve the cause of his country. He was so occupied with French revolutionary ideas as to declare himself as 'Citizen Tipu', started a Jacobin Club at his court and planted a 'Republican' tree outside his palace. In history, it is not always a success that deserves notice, but the presence of a new idea, which has the capacity of far-reaching results, also deserves recognition. His dream of a 'Republic' came through about 150 years later when India ushered into a new era on January 26, 1950.

# CHAPTER 18
# Afghanistan and Iran

Tipu contacted the ruler of Afghanistan, Zaman Shah, who ascended the throne in the year 1792. Ahmed Shah Abdali, a man of great military reputation, was his grandfather. He was also like a grandfather to Tipu. Tipu had settled with Kabul in order to secure assistance before dominating Zaman Shah.

He had written in 1790-91 to Timur Shah, the Father of Zaman Shah and to the ministers of the Court seeking military aid. In 1796, two ambassadors were sent to Kabul to tempt Shah to undertake his attack on Delhi and rescue the Mughal Emperor and to form an association with Tipu against the English. Shah reacted positively to Tipu's request and said that he would very soon carry out his aim of releasing the Mughal Emperor from the English hands.

Zaman Shah moved towards India in December 1798 and came as far as Lahore, when in January 1799 he had to return back from Kabul because in the meanwhile, the English had planned a strict action by suggesting two Persians to attack Afghanistan in his absence.

Wellesley had sent off a Shia from Moradabad to Iran who had excited Shia-Sunni differences. He had successfully prevented the awaiting danger.

Tipu was frustrated in his efforts to organize a grand group action against the English

Tipu had contacts with Iran as well. In 1797, the Prince of Iran, having quarreled with his father, arrived at Srirangapatna where he was received with self-respect and honour. Tipu lodged him in the outer reaches of Ganjam, visited him often and said at the time of his departure, "After you have made arrangements regarding the capital of the Sultanate of Persia, it is my wish that you and I jointly with Zaman Shah should attempt to shape and put in order the countries of Hindustan and Dekhan." The prince agreed to the proposal and promised to co-operate. Tipu was more concerned for building commercial relations with Iran knowing well its military weakness. He wanted to restart the old trade routes via Iran to Europe. He also wished to establish commercial centres in Iran in return for similar facilities to the Persians in Mysore.

He wrote a letter to the *Shah* of Iran and also sent an agent, Nurullah to make an impact on the Shah of the importance of Political and Commercial contacts. Here also the British defeated Tipu's planning by exciting Shia-sunni differences.

So Tipu's attempts to make international contacts for his political and military format failed because of the superior skills of the British and also because of the unknown reasons like the outburst of the French Revolution. Neither the French nor the Turks nor the Afghans were ready to help Tipu. A series of circumstances caused serious obstacles in his way, while step by step they prepared the way for British dominance in India.

# CHAPTER 19
# Political Liberty

Tipu fought for long to achieve political freedom from the hands of British for which he used all his plan of action, energy and power. He said that the life of a lion for a day was far better than the life of a jackal for hundred years. Tipu was a determined and tough enemy who never made any compromises in his ideals and purpose and never surrendered himself to any foreign power. He always dreamt of having war with British. His rule began in the mid of war against the English and ended in the mid of war against them. He was the ruler who died fighting for the freedom of his land.

Tipu called for his neighbours like the Marathas and the Nizams for help. But they were so involved in their self affairs that they never responded against the British attacks and his calls.

He was upset with his Indian neighbours so he took help from the Turks, Afghans and Napoleon. Napoleon, Zaman was keen to help him but due to hurdles set by British they stepped back, yet Tipu fought for freedom and never bowed in front of the foreign rule.

# CHAPTER 20
# Technology

*Rocket*

During the 18th Century, Hyder Ali, developed war rockets in India. Despite the usage of crude hammered soft iron, the use of metal cylinders to contain the burning powder gave them higher bursting strength. The rocket body was tied with leather thongs to a long bamboo stick. Its range was more than a kilometre. They have special effects against armed troops and were thrown into the air after lighting the dry hard ground.

Hyder Ali's son Tipu Sultan continued the development and growth of rocket weapons. He allegedly increased the number of rocket troops from 1200 to 5000. In the battles of Seringapatam in 1792 and 1799 these rockets were used against the British army.

Tipu always defeated the British for long with his own power. But he could not overcome their game and plots. So he was defeated in his capital Seringapatam and compelled to sign a shameful treaty on 22, 1792. As a result he had to give in half of his kingdom and pay a compensation of rupees 33 million to the British and their partners.

The union between the opponents was soon broken and in 1795, the British, after defeating the Nizam, once again turned their attention towards Mysore. After the treaty at Seringapatam, Tipu Sultan did not waste his time in preparing himself well against the British. He had rebuilt his war machines in the shorter possible time with the help of the French. The British regarded it as disobedience of the treaty. This resulted in the beginning of the fourth Anglo Mysore war in 1798 with the help of the Nizam. The French were unable to provide support to Tipu Sultan. Tipu Sultan moved away to his capital and continued fighting till his last breath in May 1799. Tipu Sultan was buried at a burial chamber that he himself had built, along with his father Hyder Ali and his mother Fatima Begum.

# CHAPTER 21
# Tipu's Government

Tipu was a true patriot, he could make out that the British management was growing stronger. He was a kind and peaceful ruler though he spent most of his days fighting with the Marathas, Nizams and British. He was an open-minded emperor. Many roads, tanks and dams were constructed during his rule. He promoted agriculture and supported new industries, trade and commerce.

Tipu banned the production and distribution of liquor and other intoxicants in Mysore. He also built large forts and many beautiful palaces, which were destroyed by the British after his death but the Bangalore Summer Palace still survives and is a footprint of his glorious rule.

Great moments of history are not when empires were built, but it is when human mind develop, nourish, cherish and defend the highest values of life. History is the unfolding drama of human, political, social, cultural and economic freedom.

Tipu lived and died to support the values of these freedoms.

He used all his means, energy, strength, resources and his life for the freedom of the land.

His short but stormy rule was exciting in many respects but its main importance in life is his strong enmity towards the British in India. In the history of India, Tipu was a great soldier, who deserves to be remembered as the one who sacrificed his life for the freedom of India.

# CHAPTER 22
# Timeline of Tipu's Life

*Childhood and parentage*

Tipu was born in Devanahalli (in Karnataka), on Friday, November 20th, 1753. At the age of fifteen he went on Military campaigns with his father. He was a devout Muslim and a learned man. He had a very inquisitive mind and fascination for learning His personal library consisted of more than two thousand books in different languages. Tipu was a man of simple habits leading a holy life. He impressed the people who came in contact with him with his grand personality. He was an extremely active man and worked day and night for the wellbeing of his subjects. He took over the kingdom after his father's death in 1782 A.D.

*Fighting the British*

He could foretell that the (British) East India

Company was going to capture the Indian soil from its very roots. But as a true patriotic warrior he vowed to erase them from the soil. For this purpose he dealt with the Frenchmen and even sheltered the Frenchmen who preached the French revolutionary ideologies to the public.

A 'Jacobean Club' was established in Tipu's capital Srirangapatna and the French tricolor was hoisted. He also sought assistance from the Amir of Afghanistan and the Sultan of Turkey. He had already defeated the British at Wandiwash in 1783. The British were very scared of Tipu's growing strength and they formed an agreement with the Nizam of Hyderabad and Marathas of Maharashtra .

The French left Tipu after signing of the 'Versailles Treaty' in Europe in 1783 when the American war of Independence ended.

As long as the British fought alone, Tipu always defeated them. But he was no match for their plans. Thus he was defeated in his Capital of Srirangapatna and forced to sign a humiliating treaty on March 22nd, 1792, which resulted in granting half of his kingdom and paying of a fine of thirty million rupees. All these wars left his treasure empty and thus he was forced to surrender two of his sons to the conquerors. Governor General Cornwallis took away these two youngsters to his headquarters at Calcutta in Bengal. However, they could not let down Tipu's spirits for long and he rebuilt his war machine within short time and also built a fine army and modernized his government on the European model.

# CHAPTER 23
## Tipu's Skill

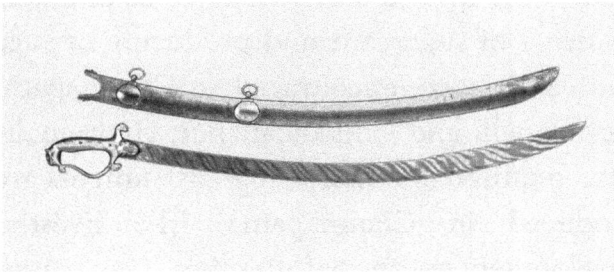

Tipu Sultan constructed tanks and dams to promote agriculture. He introduced the new industries, promoted trades and commerce, established factories in Cutch, Masquat and Jeddah and sent commercial officials to Oman, Persia and Turkey. He invited foreign skill men to build factories to produce glass, mirrors and ship-building goods. He aimed at making his kingdom the most prosperous state of India.

Hence he was also interested in latest scientific research all over the world. He introduced sericulture on a large scale and mulberry cultivation was started at twenty one centres. He encouraged the textile industry by banning the export of cotton. The weavers from Tamil Nadu were invited and settled in his kingdom. Growing of sugarcane and producing of sugar and candy were encouraged in Channapatna, Devanahalli and Chikkaballapur. High quality wire required for the string instruments was produced in Channapatna. The livestock development got special attention. Tipu banned the production and distribution of liquor and other intoxicants in his state of Mysore.

Tipu Sultan adopted the tiger as his emblem. His throne was shaped like a tiger, carrying the head of a life-size tiger in solid gold. He was an educated ruler who treated his subjects generously. He appointed non-Muslims to different positions of authority and gave them complete freedom of worship. He granted freedom and funds to Sringeri, Srirangapatna and Mangalore temples and presented them with gold and silver for the idols. He also encouraged learning of all forms of arts & crafts, music and dance etc.

Tipu's popularity among his subjects and in the neighborhood states were dismay for the English. Hence they decided to finish him once forever. The fourth Srirangapatna war came very handy to them to exterminate Tipu on May 4th, 1799. A small monument has been erected where his dead body was found.

Tipu also had a good collection of weapons, but a particular sword was his favourite. He fought his last war with the same sword. When he was critically injured, a British intended to snatch away the weapon, but Tipu killed him with the same sword, which was his precious possession. The victorious General Harris sent Tipu's war-horse, the palanquin and a howdah to the king of Coorg who was at British side.

After capturing most of the Tipu's territory, the famous sword was sent to London. This was brought back after India's Independence (1947) but was about to be smuggled out of the country when it was stopped and was preserved in the country.

### *Tipu, the builder*

The most famous and beautiful art unit from Tipu Sultan's period is his Summer palace, the Daria Daulat. It beautifully describes some of the heroic wars that Tipu fought and also depicts many social themes of the period.

Tipu built the 'Gumbaz' at Srirangapatna in 1784, which is a square shaped mausoleum with ivory doors and black marble pillars. Tipu is buried here by the side of his father Hyder Ali and mother Fatima Begum. Outside the tomb are the graves of his relatives and commanders. Nearby the 'Mashit-e-Aqsa' mosque, with a pair of small minarets is located. A solar clock could be found outside this building.

Tipu built and captured large number of forts, but unfortunately most of them are either destroyed or are in ruins because of poor maintenance. The Bangalore fort, located in the heart of the city has a temple of Lord Ganesha where devotees offer prayers regularly. His Bangalore Summer Palace is a great tourists' attraction. It is completely made of wooden structures with five well decorated and painted arches.